ounces

Poems

cionn

LOUD
SPEAKER
PRESS

Do not grieve. Anything you lose comes round in another form.

— Rumi

12:26 am

Ounces is an offering meant to feel like a conversation that sometimes looks like a confession. I started writing it around 4 a.m., in the quiet stretch after my fortieth birthday in 2024. The world was asleep on a Christmas high, having another, feeling fine or pretending to be. I wasn't. I was sitting with that number. Not the party version of forty. The weight version. The kind that shows up when the room goes quiet and you stop performing for a minute.

I let the noise inside slow down just enough to hear what was underneath. Some of it came out in a notebook. A lot of it came out as notes on my phone. A few early drafts lived for a while as voice memos untitled, identifiable only by a timestamp. Half-formed thoughts recorded in the dark. I wasn't trying to write a book. I was trying to make sense of what I was carrying. That's where these poems started. Not as poems, really. As fragments. Observations. Questions I didn't have answers to but couldn't stop asking.

A way of taking inventory not just of the world around me, but of how much time I might have left, and what I'd been doing with the time I'd already spent. The first complete poem was the title piece, Ounces. It came that same night.

Forty sat heavy on my chest. I'm from New York, and while pouring out a 40 was never my ritual, I understood the symbolism loss, remembrance, release. The act of acknowledging what's been carried and what can't be carried anymore. That's what this book became. A way of pouring out what I was holding, without pretending it disappears once it leaves my hands. Nine poems.

Not a lot. I kept it there on purpose. Not too neat. Not too complete. Enough to hold weight, and enough to leave room. Some of these poems are quiet. Interior. The kind of writing that happens when you're sitting with yourself at an hour nobody else is awake for. You might feel like we're in the same room when you read them. That's intentional. Other poems turn outward. Pieces like hold the ice and the volume pay closer attention to the world we're all navigating systems, surveillance, noise, pressure. They ask how much of ourselves we're expected to carry just to move through a day. Where some poems sit with reflection, these sit with tension. With proximity. With what happens when your private life collides with public reality.

We're living in a post-pandemic reality where everyone seems exposed and numbed at the same time. There's an anonymous grief that still hangs around. Systems crack. People crack. And most of us are holding something we haven't named yet anxiety, fear, loneliness, vulnerability, power. All of it pressed into the same body, the same commute, the same screen. These poems come from that space. Not as autobiography. Not as a rant about my life.

They're written toward what we share. The things that press on us from different angles but land in familiar places. I wrote them for the times when I couldn't look away anymore from myself, or from the world we're moving through together. You might see yourself here. You might not. Either way, you're invited to sit with them as they are unfinished, unresolved, alive. Art doesn't need to explain itself to be honest. It just needs to be felt however your feel it. These are my ounces. What you do with them is yours. Thanks for being here.

Tell me, what is it you plan to do with your one wild and
precious life?

— Mary Oliver

For the ones that love me, I love you too. Every moment, the good ones, the bad ones, and the in-between ones are an extraordinary gift from God. Lessons are learned, and blessings held. Some memories float away, and my heartfelt thanks remains.

To my readers: we don't know each other yet, but I wrote this with you in mind, with the hope that you will know me through these fragile, funny and sometimes full of shit words of mine.

contents

1
trigger(ed) finger

They say I should come with a warning.
Well… consider yourself warned.

You will get triggered
like steel beneath a cop's finger,
tight on the trigger,
his gaze steady,
gun already aimed.
Behind green eyes.

That kind of triggered.
Sweaty palms.
Heart pounding.
Breath caught
between fight and collapse.
No
I don't know how long
my composure will last.
Breaking down.
Yeah…
that trigger.

See,
poetry ain't always pretty.
But it should always be honest.
I can't let my honesty
rot on the sidelines,
locked in my skull,
when too many of you
are feeling me.

This
this is therapy.
Not just for me.
For you.
For him.
For her.
For all of us
trapped in chambers.

There's too much going on.
Too much pretending.
Too much pain
painted over.

And when you search for truth,
you don't just find truth.
You find lies
socialized as truth,
clinging like shadows.

And honestly?
I wonder why the truth
still triggers me.

They taught me conformity.
Sold it as normality.
But it's not normal for me.
Is it normal for you?

It's not normal
to live in an echo chamber,
bullshit ricocheting off walls
like a bullet in a barrel.

Sweaty palms.
Heavy legs from running
but running from what?
From myself?
From the sound of my own voice?

What's my defense
if I can't even defend myself
with words?

So yeah
you'll be triggered
like that steel click
beneath the press of a finger.

Criminal.
That trigger.

Triggered at
until I can't even accept
that maybe it's not all bad
except, it is that bad.
And sometimes worse.

I mistook determination
for wisdom,
recycled opinions for vision,
until it clouded me,
crowded out
the real adversary.

So yeah,
you'll get triggered.
Like that pew pew
resting in government's palm.
That Glock.
That Sig.
That brand
of fear.

And I'm reimagining
what it means to be a man.
If my hands are empty,
am I still a man?

Hear me.
They told me
there's a right to bear arms.
But whose arms?
And whose right?
Will it all go left?

*So prepare yourself
to be triggered.*

*Prepare
to be
triggered.*

I'm only a finger.

2
knock.

Knock.
Who
Is
He

When I am you,
and you are he,
I guess we are a lost reality.

Reality, doesn't check.
Reality, a chin check.

Seriously.
It's scary out there
in here.

Knock.
Knock.
Reality, motherfucker,

I'm here to beat your
ass,
With the truth's broke handle,
Made-up facts.

I had to check myself in,
like a self-imposed rehab,
as I slip into
habilitation. Hallucinations.

I couldn't live with myself
or you, too.

Me too?

Knock.
Who is he?
Knock.

And why is his face distorted, broken
He wears lived in cracks
a reflection,
Lost perception peek-a-boo'd in my chest.

Palpitations
emotional masturbation.
Feeding my illusions
with both hands.

Yeah, I was fucking with myself.
In a nut-shell,
I didn't treasure my youth,
but invested in the negative.

Heartbreak leads to
negative.
Heartbreak looks like healing
behind green eyes,
cracked visions
through the smile
of a sad man.

Knock.
Who
Yoo-who.
Have a drink

Uncomfortable?
Really?

Reality,
a pain in the ass,
a sat thumbtack.

Attacks of unrealistic expectations,
of anxiety.
Panic,
wrapped in myself.

Reality,
Moved to the shelf
with the books I don't read.

See
I couldn't.
Didn't.
Read me

like thick glasses,
Not strong, or ready,
The wrong prescription.
Enough already.
Scene differently

Reality made me feel
like I wasn't enough.

He was me.

But maybe I was knocking.

Knock.
Life,
Knock.
reality
And some like it rough.

I guess
I like it too, rough.
Emotionally, rough.

Toxic

I felt you weren't tough enough
since I knew.
I wasn't tough enough.

I used to,
I fought me and lost
when I was my
punching bag.

Overcoming hurts,
busted knuckles,
combined with the pleasure
of a long night of over-cumming
allowing me to come back
to myself.

Giving back,
a shot of myself.
A drop of what I was.
When I was, knocking

This reality
scaring me.
Bruising, us
Traumatizing we.

So approach
cautiously.

Willingly

Knock.
Vulnerably
Knock.
Lovingly,
Knock,
Un-seriously

Enough

Knock.

3
to go

Have a drink.
He said, pull up.
I said, pull the ice.
Put it in a cup.

To go.
Full cup.
Clear.
No transparency.
Not for me.

He said don't leave it in the car.

But I don't drive,
so stop driving me crazy.
Let me take what I paid for.

Already trained
hop the turnstile
before it turned into a style.

All black.
Not driving.

Jesus don't need the wheel.
The cup is leaking.
He put it in a double cup.

I drink it fast.

Not intoxicated
intoxicating.
Blurry-eyed.

Green suit.
Unmarked ride.
Masks, hide.

A garbage man?

Stairs down.
Underground.
Railroad.

Three dollars at a time.

Hopped the turnstile
with my drink.

I bought Fritos
from a candy lady.
Zen mentally.

Does my drink need
company or empathy?

Corner of my eye
same time.
Dude laughing.

Not me.
They called her over.

Accent.

Hands bury hands in pockets
proof of funds, paper.

Eye contact.
Hands back out.

Gold
no.
Brass.

My bad.
Plastic maybe.
A badge.

Last
ounces.

Glad I said hold the ice.
I'd be done by now.

Next stop.
Doors open.

I wasn't getting off.
Neither was the candy lady.

More than a finger
on Nutter Butters,
Butterfingers
on the floor.

Where you from?
More pressure.
Where you from?
Can't be here.

I dropped my cup.

People asked why.

Badges ignored them.

Papers.
Not snacks.
Not cash.

What country you from?
Can't be ours.

Seconds stretch.
Phone dying.

A pop.

Not snack packs.

My cup.

Double cup.
Stepped on.
Empty.

Stand clear
of the closing doors.

Pushing.
Filming.

Crying.
Pain.

My empty cup
under a boot.

Made in the USA.

Legs wobble.
Lungs heavy.
Heart loud.

Next stop announced.

Trampled.
Pushed back.

Agent Smith crashes out.
No papers.
Phones out.
For the gram.

Doors rush open.

Seconds widen.

I don't remember what I drank
running,
panting.

Me and my phone
out of juice.

Still
fuck ice.

4

emergency?

Am I in crisis?
Or am I,
a mental health crisis,
where I can't afford, help.
Yes insurance is instrumental,
my mental
don't have assurances
that coverage covers enough
I can barely cover my own, ass
where ends pretend to meet.
So I put off health care,
another year shaved from my life.
Walking into crisis,
leaning on the advice of vices.
Self-medicated gaps here,
and the doctor is nowhere.

Here

How is it a crisis
if they don't care about care?
Am I part of the system?
Am I in crisis?

Or am I
a system of checks and balances,
Unbalancing my checking account,
my paycheck,
my next check,
my rent check.
Already, spent.
Checkmate on income.
A nonexistent child support,
Abort, a broke outcome.
The rent is too damn high to stay.
Where do savings go?
Too, low
I can't afford to...
save up,
pick up,
and move up?
I can't change the prices,
To pay what the system says.
Fare,
unfair,
where,
here?

Emergency

a healthcare crisis,
an affordability crisis?
I don't believe
everything is my crisis,
so I get back to my own devices
while everyone's on their own devices,
scrolling crisis after crisis.

Identity crisis
when I'm coming and going,
doing everything on the table
like an afterparty
after the parties got my vote.
The party's over.
Crisis?

I should've known better
than an educational crisis
don't know what to believe.
They said hit my knees,
but how can a prayer stop
this crisis fucking, my head?

Am I in crisis?
Or am I

just a disaster, naturally.
Blame the victim
like a natural disaster.

Facing imposter syndrome,
I shouldn't be here
even if I can't afford
to be anywhere else.

Between here and there,
my current address is fear.

Mental health crisis,
affordability crisis,
identity crisis,
addiction crisis,
crisis of faith

I am part of the system.
My current address is fear.

And still,
this question follows me home:
Doesn't crisis mean emergency?

Emergency.
Emergency.
Emergency.

Am I in crisis?
Or am I
an emergency,
when everything else is

Emergency.
Emergency.
Emergency.

Until it all becomes
white
noise.

Am I the crisis?
Or just
the alert?

5
soliloquy of a broken condom

I am lying here
on the floor.
Unwrapped.
Unclaimed.
Unnecessary.

Am I discarded?
Naked. Used up.
A question mark in latex skin.

Can't you see I'm still full of life
just stained with it.
Still feel like I'm part of you,
even as you step out of me.

I know I'm dirty.
Drying out.
Tell me
are you my partner,
or am I yours?

At my core, I'm a single-use promise
that broke halfway through belief.
So I'll never know who the "hoe" is,
cause I was made holy
but not wholly there
holes in me before I could ever arrive
at the destiny my maker designed.

I was supposed to be your horse,
your rough rider,
your ride-or-die until the end.
Your raincoat in a storm of decisions.
Holier than most.
Disposable like the rest.

A Trojan that couldn't play horse.

I couldn't be what I wanted to be.
Couldn't be all I could be
cause the army didn't want me.

I tried to hold on
to what I hoped was meant for me,
but it only took the space
of a two-finger grip
to split me
the certainty of a pin.

How many angels fit there?

My brokenness learned time.
My structure learned surrender.
Too many holes.
A single-use whore
and a virgin at the same time.

Open. Open. Open.
Bleeding out intention.
Letting it in.
Drying out meaning.

When you throw me away

What follows?
An accident?
Or eighteen years of gravity?

When you throw me away

We weigh it on the scales
of what could've been,
might've been,
should've been
before there were holes in me.

Then comes the thrust of time:
faster. Faster. Faster.
The slam of my existence.
The insult of the present.

When you throw me away —

How can I be potential
when I'm clinging to a second hand
that snaps before it means anything?

On the whole,
in a whole,
with a hole,
through the hole
that started everything.

Why can I be so mentally weak?
How?
How?
Why now?

That was decades ago.
Millions, no,
billions of seconds ago.

Thrown away.
Forgotten.
Folded into a silence
that still remembers shape.

And this
is the soliloquy
of a broken condom.

Did I fail?

Or did I just do
what I was made to do
too honestly?

6
ounces

40 ounces of memories.,
and the ounces of bullshit I overcame...
forty heartbeats
forty panic attacks
living in my chest,
backtracking through ounces and energies,
still running through these kidneys.
Thirty-nine inhaled,
steps.
thirty-eight, and making the same mistakes,
thirty-seven risks to take.
40 ounces of memories.

Thirty-seven lost jackets, promises,
and lighters.
Kissed thirty-six cigarettes
behind forgotten joints,
thirty-five dreams run from me.
40 ounces of memories.

Thirty-four, thirty-three, thirty-two...
times I couldn't get out of bed.
I'm still in bed,
judging me.
A sip can't hold me!
40 ounces of memories.

Thirty-one times I wanted to call home
but couldn't find the number,
Thirty pills flushed,
Half confessions to everyone.
40 ounces of memories.

Twenty-nine parties,
twenty-eight drinks too many,
twenty-seven exes to bury in the past,
twenty-six broken plans,
twenty-five stops on the train,
passing like twenty-four hours
after a one night stand.
40 ounces of memories.

Remembering twenty-three unanswered calls
Missed twenty-too and the calls I didn't,
want to pick up for.
Twenty-one promises to God, unkept.
Twenty times, twenty times
I tried to run from myself and got nowhere.
40 ounces of memories.

Nineteen, eighteen, seventeen:
apologies, regrets, and scars
different faces in different mirrors,
mirror mirror energy.
Sixteen love letters I never wrote.
Fifteen birthdays I forgot on purpose.
Fourteen, thirteen trips to forget
Twelve times I couldn't read the room.
Eleven times I thought you were someone else.
Ten dollars in my pocket.
40 ounces of memories.

Nine, eight, seven versions of me
buried with good intentions,
sad songs, jealousy, and empathy.
Six, I mistook getting by for a lifestyle.
Five times I thought I couldn't go on.
Four friends that became family,
and three that forgot my name.

Two fists that tried to fight the world,
one empty bottle,
Two cents,
one wish,
One father,
Many father figures,
One broken condom,
No fucks left to give
No more sips to share,
and one more breath, kept.

40 ounces of memories.

7
thoughts
& prayers

I'm scrolling.
Thumb numb.
Another headline breaks open the screen.

Another vigil.
Another mic speaks too close to grief.

They say thoughts and prayers
like it's a period
no apology.

Candles flicker.
Policies stay bulletproof.
Communities cry for shelter
round after round
leaders duck behind the cover of
thoughts
and prayers.

We pray loud enough to trend.
Quiet enough to not change shit.

Money speaks fluently.
Children learn silence early.
Why do tax dollars find war so easily
but only fund restraint
when taxpayers need saving?

Thoughts and prayers.

Say the shooter's name
fame kills more than once.
Say the victims' names never.
Algorithms crown villains.
The dead become background noise
in the room.

Doom scrolling.

Views go up.
Profits spike.
Death refreshes on a loop
inside the news cycle.

And every time we spiral
Will this be the one?
They hand us the same ballot box of air.

We vote with
thoughts
and

(no)
we don't.
Pray.

Memorials scrape the sky.
Faces ironed flat on t-shirts.
Posters peel in the rain.
Grief is merch.

Death on sale.

Poets type faster.
Feeds move quicker.
Bodies stay still.

How many bleed?
How many active shooters on go
on go.

Do we stop rehearsing sympathy
and practice responsibility?

I scroll again.
Another headline.
Another prayer.

Still no action.

Only a ballot.

8
the volume

Turn up
when you know the volume got turned down,
and the message gets turned around
to the beat of algorithms.

Vacuumed up
the context of content,
where free speech gets more costly
in the subtext of the comments,
bought by advertisers and oligarchs.

Your commentary can't run contrary
to sponsored messages
spawning from wallets and accounts
of those cashing in,
your data
Checks, flow
income streams,
streamed back to you.
Check, your history

So yeah, turn up
so your voice won't become
the white noise of statistics,
broken down by data brokers.

Who did you date,
who did you vote for,
go broke for,
and when did you fuck—for fuck's sake.

How many times a week.
Time to track your sleep.
Sell you shit on the nights you can't sleep.

And I can't sleep.
Guess my apps will find subscriptions for me.

What's the world coming to
ads during pornography,
politics as reality TV,
asking me how big I want the titties
on my AI girlfriend.

It never ends.
I guess it depends
on if you go broke first,
die and go un-alive first.

Naw
the volume got turned down already.

So let your apathy turn into
what you can no longer give:
money,
time,
And empathy

Take away all the fucks
you already gave,
except the one you saved
in your back pocket for later.

Do me a favor.
Don't get lost in the volume.

9
pour.
ring. out.

*He's at the point
in his therapy
where the ounces start
talking back.*

*Pouring out.
Drowning in.
Ringing out.
Waterboarding.
Pour that outside.*

*He says it's supposed to help,
to rinse out the inner ache.
Dark rum. Everclear. Water
was he ever there?
Not going out there.
Agoraphobia.
Ounces of open air.
In here,
drowning,
open hands,
eyes closed,
open mouth.*

Bullshit.

He can't believe the outside,
so he tries to cleanse the inside.

Outside,
people see the skin he's in.
Outside,
they call it healing.
Outside,
they don't see him drown.
Outside,
hands grasping for air, dealing

Submerged in a memory,
over his head,
under his skin,
baptizing his own pain.
The therapist says, let it pour.
He hears, let it drown.

Ounces. Lungs.
Lungs. Ounces.
Ounces. Lungs.

He keeps pouring,
ringing out,
ripping into
every old thought
that clings like wet cloth, muslin

Waterboard.

Outside,
they think he's clean.

Waterboard.

Inside, tortured,
he knows he's hollowed.

Waterboard.
Waterboard.
Waterboard.

How much of your life
can you wash away
before you start to disappear?

He's at the point
in his therapy
where he's pouring out,
baptized,

poured,
drowned,
waterboarded,
and drunk

on his own reflection.

Pour.
Ring.
Out.

3:36 am

So you made it to the end, it's after 3 am my time. For you maybe this isn't an end at all maybe it's the start of something you'll carry with you. That isn't for me to know, it's time to sleep. You know me better now, or at least you've felt some of what I've poured into these pages. These poems aren't meant to answer your questions, but they can be an answer. When I started writing I couldn't stop.

This set of poems offers more questions too. That's up to you to answer. If you found something here something fragile, something heavy, something familiar I hope you let it rest in your hands and resolve in your heart.

We measure our lives in ounces sometimes. Small weights of air, liquid, smoke, and thought that feel enormous and unwieldy when held close. Even when they overflow, even when they slip from our grip, they remind us: we were here. We lived. We are human. Thank you for taking these ounces with you.

about the author

Cionn is a visually impaired poet, editor, and visual artist from Brooklyn. He writes in the quiet hours when the world is asleep or pretending to be. His work moves between poetry, spoken word, and sound mediums where vulnerability becomes power and silence carries weight. He has spent years learning his voice, playing with form, experimenting with what poetry could hold. Ounces is different. It's the work he's proud to wear.

Nine poems written in a post-pandemic moment where everything feels exposed and numb at once. They're measurements of what we're all carrying in our bodies, our systems, our silence.